An In
Sensible Alcohol

2nd Edition

An Introduction to Sensible Alcohol Use

2nd Edition

Marcantonio Spada

ROBINSON • LONDON

ROBINSON

First published in Great Britain in 2017 by Robinson

1 3 5 7 9 10 8 6 4 2

A CIP catalogue record for this book
is available from the British Library.

Important note
This book is not intended as a substitute for medical advice
or treatment. Any person with a condition requiring medical
attention should consult a qualified medical practitioner
or suitable therapist.

ISBN: 978-1-47213-855-2

Typeset in Bembo by Initial Typesetting Services, Edinburgh
Printed and bound in Great Britain by
CPI Group (UK), Croydon CR0 4YY

Papers used by Robinson are from well-managed forests
and other responsible sources.

MIX
Paper from
responsible sources
FSC
www.fsc.org   FSC® C104740

Robinson
An imprint of
Little, Brown Book Group
Carmelite House
50 Victoria Embankment
London EC4Y 0DZ

An Hachette UK Company
www.hachette.co.uk

www.littlebrown.co.uk

Contents

About This Book

This book is aimed at helping you use alcohol in a sensible way. Part 1 describes what sensible alcohol use involves and how you can monitor and think about changing your drinking habits. Part 2 looks at the methods you can use to help you use alcohol in a sensible way.

Working through this book from beginning to end, and becoming confident in using the techniques described will take time and effort. With practice you should become increasingly confident that you can drink in a sensible way, keep up your good work and know how to deal with any setbacks. Many of the strategies in this book are based on a psychological treatment called Cognitive Behavioural Therapy, a practical, down-to-earth approach which has a successful record of helping people in distress transform their lives. You've nothing to lose by working through this book. However, you may find that you still need a helping hand. If this is the case, I would advise you to consult your GP and/or a Cognitive Behavioural Therapy practitioner who can offer you extra support.

Professor Marcantonio Spada

Part 1: SENSIBLE ALCOHOL USE

1

Setting the Scene

People drink for a range of reasons, and in varying amounts, but primarily because they like the taste and the effects of alcohol and because drinking is a social activity. Throughout the UK almost every person has access to a local pub or bar and 90 per cent of adults drink alcohol on a regular basis. For most adults then, drinking is a well-established and acceptable part of their life. Indeed drinking a small amount of alcohol does no harm and can be enjoyable.

Why Do We Drink?

The straight answer to this question is: 'Because we have learned to do so'. Chances are that you learned to drink as part of growing up in a particular culture in which the social influences of family members, friends, partners and the media shaped your behaviour and beliefs relating to alcohol. For example, you may have watched your parents reaching for a drink to relax in the evening or to give them confidence to socialize at a party. When socializing with friends you may have felt left out if you didn't have a drink and when watching TV you may have come across stories that make it seem as if drinking can help sexual prowess and make someone seem more powerful or cool.

Another reason we drink is because of our biological makeup: we're 'wired' to engage in behaviours that gratify us and drinking alcohol does just that. The reward we get from alcohol is actually twofold. Firstly, it can help us relax and make us feel less inhibited and secondly it can numb negative emotions like anxiety and low mood.

What Happens if We Drink Too Much?

Let's look at Evelyn's story:

Evelyn's story

Evelyn is a 28-year-old lawyer. She is energetic and ambitious and often works a 40 to 50 hour week. Recently, work pressures have been mounting and she's noticed that her drinking has increased. She now finds it difficult to unwind and socialize without having a drink. She has also noticed that her mood is getting worse and she doesn't sleep as well as she used to. She's beginning to wonder whether it is time to consider changing her drinking habits before they get out of hand.

When we start drinking in an unwise way we open ourselves to a variety of potential problems. Firstly, though alcohol will make us feel more relaxed and less inhibited in the short-term it will actually trigger anxiety and low mood in the medium to long-term. Secondly, because alcohol is a powerful drug, even in moderate quantities it will cause a degree of physical and psychological dependence (a state in which the use of alcohol becomes necessary for your physical and psychological well-being). Thirdly, it can put our lives at risk in two ways:

- Accidents – Alcohol impairs our ability to concentrate and also to judge speed. It slows down reaction times and blurs vision, and makes us less able to control our movements. No wonder it is linked to 35,000 deaths per year, which is almost 15–20 times more than are caused by the misuse of all illegal drugs combined. Causes of death include car accidents, drowning, falls, fires, hypothermia and poisoning.

- Medical problems – If even moderately unwise drinking habits go on long enough, our
bodies will start to experience medical problems. These may take from days to decades
to develop. You may recognise some of the
short-term effects such as anaemia, diarrhoea,
dry skin, upset stomach and pins and needles.
Long-term effects include acid reflux, cancer,
cirrhosis, cognitive impairment (problems with
attention, learning, thinking and memory),
foetal alcohol syndrome in pregnant women,
gastritis, hepatitis, impotence in men, pancrea-
titis and ulcers.

2

Understanding What
is Sensible Alcohol Use

In the UK, the Department of Health recommends that sensible drinking limits are no more than 14 units per week for both men and women spread across the week, and with at least two alcohol-free days. However, it is not a good idea to consistently drink 3 or more units a day, and if you drink regularly, you should try to have at least two alcohol-free days a week.

It is thought that drinking 1 or 2 units of alcohol a day may help to prevent coronary heart disease for men over 40 and women who have been through the menopause (but it is possible that this may cause other bad side effects for some people in these two groups). If you're pregnant or trying to become pregnant, you shouldn't drink at all.

There are some situations when it is advisable not to drink at all:

•   If you're taking certain medications, because

the effects of alcohol can be very dangerous if mixed with these. Check with your GP.

- If your GP advises you not to drink at all.
- Before you plan to drive or when you are driving.
- Before or when you're operating electrical or mechanical equipment or machinery.
- When you're at work.
- Before or during swimming or other active sports.

What is a Unit of Alcohol?

Different types of drinks contain different strengths of alcohol, so some will have more units than others. You can work out the amount of alcohol in any drink if you know the quantity of liquid and the percentage of alcohol it contains. A guide to the number of units contained in some popular drinks is below.

TYPE OF DRINK	QUANTITY	NUMBER OF UNITS
Normal strength lager/bitter/cider (Boddingtons, Carling, Harp)	Can, pint or 33cl–50cl bottle	2
Strong lager/ bitter/cider (Corona, Kronenbourg, Red Stripe, Stella)	Can, pint or 33cl–50cl bottle	3
Normal strength cider (Strongbow, Woodpecker)	1 litre bottle	4–5
Strong cider (White Lightning)	1 litre bottle	8
Alcopop (Bacardi Breezer, Smirnoff Ice, WKD)	33cl bottle	2
Sherry (Harveys Bristol Cream, QC)	75cl bottle	15

Port	75cl bottle	15
Wine	75cl bottle	7–9
Wine	250ml large pub glass	3
Wine	175ml regular pub glass	2
Brandy, gin, whisky, vodka	Single pub measure	1.4
Brandy, gin, whisky, vodka	Standard size bottle	26–28
Brandy, gin, whisky, vodka	1 litre bottle	40

3

Knowing about Your Drinking Habits

A helpful way to get an accurate picture of your drinking habits is to monitor them closely. You can do this quite easily by keeping a record of the times you've had a drink, and then noting down how much you drank, where and with whom. The drinking diary below (Drinking Diary 1) can be used to record your drinking habits. The diary below it (Drinking Diary 2) shows an example of a completed diary. It's a good idea to monitor your drinking habits for at least two weeks before moving on to Part 2 of this book.

What to Look Out For

In different situations you may tend to drink more, drink moderately or not drink at all. This is not a coincidence. Your environment can really influence your drinking, particularly if you aren't aware of it. The factors detailed on pages 16–19 will typically influence how much you drink.

DRINKING DIARY 1							
Date	Morning	Units	Afternoon	Units	Evening	Units	Total Units
Monday							
Tuesday							
Wednesday							

				Total units this week:
Thursday				
Friday				
Saturday				
Sunday				

DRINKING DIARY 2							
Date	Morning	Units	Afternoon	Units	Evening	Units	Total Units
Monday			At the pub with friends.	3	At home alone watching TV.	5	8
Tuesday					Dinner with workmates.	4	4
Wednesday							

Day				Total
Thursday		Pub with friends. 4	Alone at home doing little. 3	7
Friday		Pub with friends. 7		7
Saturday		Pub with friends. 5	Dinner with Lisa. 4	9
Sunday	Lunch with Robert. 2			2

Total units this week: 37

Places

It may be obvious to you where you are more likely to drink more, but a place can also have a subtle effect on your drinking. Research has shown, for example, that people are more likely to drink heavily in places where:

- Competition is high for sexual partners, such as in a nightclub.
- Other people are drinking heavily.
- The lights are turned down, such as in a dimly lit bar or restaurant.

If you realise that there are certain places where you're likely to drink too much, you may wish to consider avoiding them for a while. Indeed, people who successfully control their drinking often avoid these 'high-risk' places for a period of time. This doesn't mean you'll never go back to these places, but rather that if you do go back it will be when you're equipped with techniques that will allow you to drink in a sensible way. The following are practical steps you can take to break drinking habits in specific places:

- If you're going out ensure you take somebody with you who is unlikely to drink or will make it harder for you to drink.

- If you're going out do so at a time of the day and/or week that is different from usual.
- If you're at home, change your surroundings (decoration, furniture, lighting).
- Keep only limited amounts of alcohol at home.

Time

Time is an important factor in drinking habits. Most people who drink too much will do so on certain days of the week and at certain times of the day. Evenings, weekends, holidays and special occasions (e.g. parties and weddings) are likely to involve heavier drinking. Your Drinking Diary will give you an idea of the dates and times you tend to drink. A key tip is to put a firm time limit on your drinking. For example make a decision never to drink before 7 p.m. at night during the week, and 9 p.m. at night on weekends. If you do this, don't forget to avoid speeding up your drinking to compensate.

People

Being around certain people can make it more likely that you'll drink excessively. People who drink heavily will sometimes make fun of those who don't drink as much as them. They may also push drinks on you or buy extra rounds, increasing the likelihood that you'll consume more drinks than you intend to do. In other cases your drinking may be affected by the way you feel around certain people. You may feel anxious and drinking can be a way to unwind and relax. Sometimes drinking simply happens because of what you do with a particular person. If, for example, you're with a person who likes to go from pub to pub it will be harder to avoid drinking or to limit your drinking.

There are also people who you're more likely to drink moderately with. These will include people who don't drink at all, moderate drinkers, or simply people you don't feel anxious with. There may be times when you make a conscious decision to drink less because you want to make a favourable impression (e.g. with your boss).

There are a variety of things you can do if you find out that you tend to drink more in the company of certain people:

- Try to cut down your drinking and see what happens – the other person may also start reducing the amount they drink.
- Ask for help – this will mean letting your companion know that you're trying to cut down on your drinking.

•   Spend less time together – if you do this make sure that you explain that it is not to do with not liking the person but because you need to avoid places where you find you're tempted to drink.

Thoughts and Emotions

The Drinking Diary in this book will help you work out the amount of alcohol you're drinking and give you an approximate idea of what you're doing, where you are and who you're with when you drink. However, a more detailed record will help you identify the thoughts and emotions that lead you to drink. Let's look at the Trigger Record below.

As you've seen in the example above, thoughts and emotions triggered in specific situations can bring about drinking. If you keep a detailed record of this kind for a few weeks, you'll begin to see clear patterns in your own drinking habits and how they're linked to your thoughts and emotions.

TRIGGER RECORD

Date	Time	Drink	Amount	Situation	Thoughts	Emotions
5/8	18.30	Wine	2 glasses	At home before going out.	'A drink will make me relaxed.'	Excitement.
5/8	20.00	Wine	6 glasses	Talking to people at the restaurant.	'I don't like these people; I feel uncomfortable.'	Frustration. Boredom.
5/8	23.00	Whisky	2 shots	At home alone.	'Another wasted evening!'	Anger. Loneliness.

Is this Book for Me?

From your Drinking Diary you'll be able to work out if you're exceeding the recommended weekly amount of 14 units per week for both men and women spread across the week, and with at least two alcohol-free days. If you're exceeding these limits you'll roughly fit into one of the following three categories:

UNITS CONSUMED PER WEEK	DRINKING HABIT
Between 21 units and 40 units	Hazardous
Between 41 units and 60 units	High-risk
Above 60 units	Dangerous

This book is primarily aimed at helping people who fall into the first two categories (hazardous and high-risk). If you fall into the third category (dangerous), you may still find this book useful but I recommend that you consult your GP and/or a Cognitive Behavioural Therapy practitioner for further help. It is also important to bear in mind that if you're drinking less than the weekly amount but often have more than 3–4 units per day you may still be drinking in a high-risk or dangerous manner. Having a large amount of alcohol in a single day, even if you don't go over the recommended limit during the week, can be damaging.

4

Getting Motivated to
Change Your Drinking Habits

Finding out what your drinking habits are actually like may make you feel a whole range of emotions from anger, concern, low mood and upset to a sense of excitement and determination. It's likely that you'll experience a mixture of all these emotions as well as ambivalence about whether you actually want to change your drinking habits. Ambivalence is feeling two ways about something ('I want to but I don't want to'). You may well feel ambivalent because you associate both costs and benefits with continuing to drink at the same level.

How you weigh up these costs and benefits will determine whether or not you change your drinking habits. You won't always be aware of this balancing process, and even if you're aware of it, you'll not always be able to proceed like a computer towards a rational decision! This is why ambivalence is confusing, frustrating and difficult to understand. Yet it's important to carry on, despite this obstacle, and be tolerant and patient towards any feelings of ambivalence. Ambivalence is a normal part of many aspects of life. The challenge is to find ways of strengthening our willingness to change.

The most effective way of getting motivated to change your drinking habits is to list the benefits and costs of keeping the same habits, and the benefits and costs of changing them. You can try to come up with your own list of benefits and costs, as in the example opposite.

It is inevitable that you'll experience some concerns about changing your drinking habits – most, if not all, people do. What is important to bear in mind is that it's very likely that these concerns will turn out not to be a problem.

A common concern that you may have is that changing your drinking habits will make your life seem empty or boring. Sometimes, drinking more sensibly frees up substantial amounts of thinking space and activity time, but, if this happens, the chances are that you'll be able to shift your thoughts to other matters or fill your time with other activities. Resisting the craving to drink can also be distressing and this may be a source of concern. What is important to bear in mind is that this is not usually as distressing as we think it will be. Craving can be overcome fairly quickly as we drink less

CURRENT DRINKING HABIT		SENSIBLE DRINKING HABIT	
Benefits	Costs	Benefits	Costs
Helps me unwind. Gives me a high.	Damages my health. Costs me money. It's affecting my job. It upsets my partner.	Feel better. Less money problems. Better health and sleep.	What about my friends? Will they find me boring? How will I relax?

often. Some of the techniques covered later in this book will help reduce any distress you experience linked to craving.

I hope that you'll discover as you progress through this book that changing your drinking habits is not as daunting as it may at first appear.

Part 2: TECHNIQUES FOR SENSIBLE ALCOHOL USE

5

Gaining Control

If you've been drinking unwisely for a long time, learning or re-learning how to drink in a sensible way involves basic techniques, which may not be that familiar to you. The most important technique of all for keeping within the limits that you set for yourself is to slow down with your drinking. It takes some time for alcohol to take effect. This is why, if you're drinking fast, you may well be feeling the effect of the second drink while you're having your third or fourth. Consequently you may become convinced that it takes three or four drinks to get the effect you like when in reality it doesn't.

Another important reason to slow down is to ensure you adjust your tolerance to alcohol. Tolerance (being able to hold your drink) is *not* a good thing. The more tolerance you have, the larger the amount of alcohol you'll need to drink to experience the same effects. Over time, tolerance changes in relation to what you drink. When you drink more, your tolerance increases and as you cut back your tolerance decreases.

Some tips you may find useful for achieving greater control over your drinking are outlined below:

BEFORE DRINKING

Eat something beforehand.

Postpone going out.

Don't drink in places where you have previously drunk heavily.

Don't take much money with you.

Take non-alcoholic drinks with you.

Avoid going out with heavy drinkers.

Start drinking later in the day.

Set a drinking limit and ensure you check that you're sticking to it.

WHILST DRINKING

Start off with a long soft drink.

Have smaller glasses (half-pints and small wine glasses).

Dilute your alcoholic drinks.

Drink in sips so that you drink more slowly.

Switch between non-alcoholic and alcoholic drinks.

Avoid standing at the bar.

Don't eat crisps and peanuts as they'll make you thirsty.

Practise refusing a drink.

Distract yourself whilst drinking (e.g. play darts, have a chat).

Try to go home early.

A Controlled Drinking Programme

The following is a brief drinking programme (for a typical week) that you can use as a template for your own programme:

This programme should translate into no more than two to three drinks per day and two to three days a week without drinking. Don't forget to continue self-monitoring what you actually drink. This is important for two reasons: firstly, it'll give you a better idea of what you're actually drinking; and secondly, it'll make you aware if something is not going the way it should (i.e. you're over-drinking).

KEY TARGETS	WHAT TO REMEMBER	STRATEGIC PLAN
1. Three days a week without a drink.	1. Alcohol-free days are Tuesday, Thursday and Sunday.	1. Eat something before I go out.
2. No drinking before 7 p.m.	2. I tend to drink more when I drink wine so stick to beer.	2. Don't take more than £10 with me.
3. No more than 3 units per day.		3. Practise refusing a drink.
		4. Always start with a soft drink.
		5. Do something when I'm there that doesn't involve only drinking.

It is important to bear in mind that it can be harder to try and limit your drinking than to stop altogether. Stopping altogether just involves avoiding drinking alcohol. When you are attempting to control the amount you are drinking it can be easy to miscalculate how much you have drunk. You may forget what you've drunk, or even deliberately miscalculate the number of units. Also, drinking alcohol frees up our inhibitions, which means once you have had one or two, you could lose your determination to keep to your prearranged limit.

Research suggests that the following factors are likely to influence how successful you are in controlling your drinking: your age; whether you're employed; whether you have a family around you; whether you have a short, rather than long, history of drinking problems and whether you show any signs of alcohol dependence.

6

Refusing Drinks

It's inevitable that people around you will offer you drinks or pressure you to drink. Family gatherings, office parties, dates and dinners with friends are some of the settings where there will be alcohol and where you may feel pressure to drink. The pressure may come from a single casual offer of a drink to being seriously pressurized to have one. Being able to say no to a drink will require commitment and the rehearsal of drinking refusal techniques. These will allow you to respond more effectively to real-life situations when they arise. The list below describes different techniques that you can adopt when refusing drinks:

- *Voice and Eye Contact*. Refuse the drink in an unhesitant manner. Your voice will have to be clear and firm. This will help stop questions about whether you mean what you say. Ensure that you make direct eye contact with the other person, as this will increase the effectiveness of the message.

- *Change the Subject of the Conversation and Suggest an Alternative.* After refusing the drink, change the subject of conversation to avoid being drawn into a debate about drinking. You may also want to do something else, such as go for a walk or a drive, or you could suggest having something else to drink or eat (e.g. coffee or dessert).

- *Ask for a Change in Behaviour.* If the person continues to pressure you, clarify that you don't want them to offer you a drink anymore. For example, 'Thanks for offering me a drink again. I just don't want one, so please stop asking me.'

- *Avoid Excuses and Vague Answers.* 'I am not that well' or 'I usually would have one, but not tonight' will only serve to postpone having to face refusing a drink. It might also imply that at some later date you'll accept the offer of a drink, putting more pressure on both you and the person offering it. That said, in extreme cases where there is unrelenting pressure to have a drink you may end up needing to use these kinds of excuses as a last resort.

- *Rehearse.* Try to practise drinking refusal techniques before going into high-risk situations. In the example below, Helen practised refusing drinks before going to a friend's wedding reception where she knew she would be offered many drinks:

Guest: Would you like a drink?

Helen: I'll have a Coke, please.

Guest: Come on. Just one drink! It's an important day! Don't spoil it by being boring!

Helen: I'm not drinking at the moment.

Guest: Why not?

Helen: Drinking doesn't agree with me.

Guest: Why doesn't it agree with you?

Helen: There are plenty of other things we can talk about. Did you enjoy the wedding service?

7

Tackling Thoughts about Drinking

Our thoughts can affect how much we drink. Two kinds of thoughts are particularly important: positive and permissive thoughts about drinking. Positive thoughts about drinking relate to the anticipated benefits of drinking. The following are examples of positive thoughts about drinking:

- 'Drinking makes me more affectionate.'
- 'Drinking helps me to control negative thoughts.'
- 'Drinking reduces feelings of anxiety.'
- 'Drinking makes me more sociable.'
- 'Drinking helps me fit in socially.'

Permissive thoughts about drinking (also known as 'rationalising') typically involve believing that you're entitled to a drink, that there won't really be any bad consequences in drinking as well as finding acceptable excuses to have a drink. These kinds of thoughts undermine our ability to put up with craving and play an important role in keeping drinking going once we have started. The following are examples of permissive thoughts about drinking:

- 'I will just have one more drink.'
- 'I have to drink at this moment.'
- 'Another drink won't harm me.'
- 'Now that I have started drinking, I might as well carry on.'
- 'This is the last time I will be drinking so I should have all I want.'
- 'I will start afresh tomorrow.'

It is crucial to learn to spot both positive and permissive thoughts about drinking while they are happening. However, recognising these thoughts is not always straightforward and you'll need to practise. The techniques that follow will help you identify and challenge these thoughts in situations where you drink an unhealthy amount.

Identifying and Challenging Positive Thoughts about Drinking

To help you identify positive thoughts about drinking, follow the step-by-step instructions below to complete Worksheet 1B. Worksheet 1A on page 40 is an example of a completed worksheet.

- *Step 1*: Write down the trigger of your drinking episode. Run through the questions at the bottom of the table under the heading 'Trigger' in Worksheet 1B.

- *Step 2*: Under the heading 'Feelings and Sensations' write down the feelings (e.g. anxiety, low mood, sadness, worry) and sensations (e.g. heart racing, palpitations, sweating) you noticed before you started drinking.

- *Step 3*: Under the heading 'Positive Thoughts about Drinking' write down the thoughts you noticed before you started drinking. Make sure you identify the key thought (the thought that increases most your chances of starting to drink) and highlight it. Practise doing this exercise whenever possible over a period of two to three weeks. Don't forget that practice will make it easier to identify these thoughts.

WORKSHEET 1A

IDENTIFYING POSITIVE THOUGHTS ABOUT DRINKING – ABBY'S STORY

Trigger	Feelings and Sensations	Positive Thoughts about Drinking
Coming back from work, seeing the house empty and thinking of an argument I had at work.	Angry and low.	'I will feel better after a drink.' 'Drinking will help me control my negative thoughts.'
At a party, meeting new people.	Anxious.	'Drinking will make me more sociable.'

On a Friday afternoon, at a conference, I asked a poor question.	Anxious and angry.	'Drinking will make me fit in.' 'Alcohol is the only way to get rid of the anxiety and anger.'
On a Saturday afternoon, I was walking along a canal.	Bored and frustrated.	'The only way I'll have fun today is if I drink.'

WORKSHEET 1B
IDENTIFYING POSITIVE THOUGHTS ABOUT DRINKING

Trigger	Feelings and Sensations	Positive Thoughts about Drinking

When did it happen? Where were you? What were you doing? What were you thinking about?	What feelings and body sensations did you notice?	How did you think drinking would help? What were you afraid might happen if you did not drink?

Once you've identified your positive thoughts about drinking it is important to practise how to challenge them. There are eight key questions you should always ask yourself when challenging positive thoughts about drinking:

1. 'Do these thoughts make it easier or harder for me to drink?'

2. 'What would I say to someone else who had these thoughts?'

3. 'What have I learned from drinking in the past that could help me now?'

4. 'Am I being misled by my feelings?'

5. 'What are the consequences of thinking in this way?'

6. 'How will I feel later?'

7. 'What would someone else say about these thoughts?'

8. 'Is this situation similar to past situations?'

Follow the step-by-step instructions below and use Worksheet 2B on page 48 to challenge your positive thoughts about your drinking. An example of a completed worksheet can be found on page 46 (Worksheet 2A).

- *Step 1*: Just like in Worksheet 1B, write down the trigger of your drinking episode, the associated feelings and sensations, and positive thoughts about drinking. Identify the key positive thought about drinking and highlight it.

- *Step 2*: Under the heading 'Evidence Not Supporting the Thought' write down all the evidence that suggests that the thought is not true. Use the eight questions, listed above, to challenge positive thoughts about drinking.

- *Step 3*: Under the heading 'Alternative Thought' record an alternative and more balanced thought than the positive thought you originally had about drinking. Again, use the eight questions for challenging positive thoughts about drinking.

- *Step 4*: Finally, rate how much you believe the alternative thought to be true on a scale from 0 to 100, with 0 being no belief in the thought and 100 being completely convinced by the thought.

WORKSHEET 2A
IDENTIFYING AND CHALLENGING POSITIVE THOUGHTS ABOUT DRINKING – ABBY'S STORY

Trigger	Feelings and Sensations	Positive Thoughts about Drinking	Evidence Not Supporting the Thought	Alternative Thought	Belief in Alternative Thought
Coming back from work, seeing the house empty and thinking of an argument I had at work.	Angry and low.	'I will feel better after a drink.'	The good feeling doesn't last that long.	'I will feel so bad after drinking that it is better to avoid it!'	95
		'Drinking will help me control my negative thoughts.'	They still come back and usually worse after I've been drinking.	'Drinking makes me think more negatively.'	95

| At a party, meeting new people. | Anxious. | 'Drinking will make me more sociable.' | I get aggressive when I drink, which ends up ruining my evenings. | 'Drinking might make me relaxed, but it won't last for long and usually results in a mess.' | 85 |
| On a Friday afternoon, at a conference, I asked a poor question. | Anxious and angry. | 'Drinking will make me fit in.' | The anxiety or anger, without drinking, will go. There are positive things I can do to speed this up (e.g. talk to someone). | 'The anxiety and anger will go and I can help this along. Alcohol will make me feel worse not better. I need to break the habit of coping with negative emotions.' | 95 |

WORKSHEET 2B

IDENTIFYING AND CHALLENGING POSITIVE THOUGHTS ABOUT DRINKING

Trigger	Feelings and Sensations	Positive Thoughts about Drinking	Evidence Not Supporting the Thought	Alternative Thought	Belief in Alternative Thought

When did it happen? Where were you? What were you doing? What were you thinking about?	What feelings and body sensations did you notice?	What were you saying to your-self that made it easier to keep drinking? Highlight the key thought that makes you most likely to continue drinking.	Use the eight questions on page 44 to challenge your thought.	Note the alternative more helpful thought.	Rate how much you believe this thought to be true on a scale from 0 to 100.

Identifying and Challenging Permissive Thoughts about Drinking

To help you identify permissive thoughts about drinking use the worksheet on page 52 (Worksheet 3B) and follow the step-by-step instructions below. An example of a completed worksheet can be found on page 51 (Worksheet 3A).

- *Step 1*: Write down the trigger of your drinking episode. Run through the questions at the bottom of the table under the heading 'Trigger' in Worksheet 3B.

- *Step 2*: Under the heading 'Feelings and Sensations' write down any feelings (e.g. anxiety, low mood, sadness, worry) and sensations (e.g. heart racing, palpitations, sweating) you noticed before your drinking escalated.

- *Step 3*: Under the heading 'Permissive Thoughts about Drinking' write down all the thoughts you had before your drinking escalated. Make sure you identify the key thought (the thought that increases most your chances of continuing drinking) and highlight it. Practise doing this exercise whenever possible over the next two to three weeks. Don't forget that practice will make it easier to identify these thoughts in the future.

WORKSHEET 3A

IDENTIFYING PERMISSIVE THOUGHTS ABOUT DRINKING – STEVE'S STORY

Trigger	Feelings and Sensations	Permissive Thoughts about Drinking
On a Saturday, I was walking by myself along Regent's canal. I'd passed several pubs and off-licences. I had a strong desire to drink, so stopped and had one.	Bored, frustrated, and worried. Slightly elated from the alcohol, guilty.	'I've only got £25. So I can't do too much damage.' 'I can start afresh tomorrow.'
On one occasion recently, I went into a pub with the intention of drinking no more than two pints of beer. I drank four pints.	Bored, frustrated, and worried. Slightly elated from the alcohol, guilty.	'I've got to drink more.' 'Another few drinks won't do any harm.'

WORKSHEET 3B

IDENTIFYING PERMISSIVE THOUGHTS ABOUT DRINKING

Trigger	Feelings and Sensations	Permissive Thoughts about Drinking

		What were you saying to yourself that made it easier to keep drinking? Highlight the key thought that makes it most likely for you to continue drinking.
	What feelings and body sensations did you notice?	
When did it happen? Where were you? What were you doing? What were you thinking about?		

Once you've identified any permissive thoughts about drinking it is important to learn and to practise doing so. Return to the eight key questions you used to challenge positive thoughts about drinking (see page 44) and use them to challenge your permissive thoughts about drinking.

Use Worksheet 4B on page 58 for this exercise and follow the step-by-step instructions below. An example of a completed worksheet can be found on page 56 (Worksheet 4A).

- *Step 1*: Write down the trigger of your drinking episode and any associated feelings and sensations, and permissive thoughts about drinking. Identify your key permissive thought about drinking and highlight it.

- *Step 2*: Under the heading 'Evidence Not Supporting the Thought' write down all the evidence that suggests that the thought is not true. Use the eight questions on page 44 to challenge the permissive thoughts about drinking listed above.

- *Step 3*: Under the heading 'Alternative Thought' record an alternative and more balanced thought. Again, use the eight questions for challenging permissive thoughts about drinking.

- *Step 4*: Finally, rate how much you believe the alternative thought to be true on a scale from 0 to 100, with 0 being no belief in the thought and 100 being completely convinced by it.

WORKSHEET 4A   IDENTIFYING AND CHALLENGING
PERMISSIVE THOUGHTS ABOUT DRINKING – STEVE'S STORY

Trigger	Feelings and Sensations	Positive Thoughts about Drinking	Evidence Not Supporting the Thought	Alternative Thought	Belief in Alternative Thought
On a Saturday, I was walking by myself along Regent's canal. I'd passed several pubs and off licences. I had a strong desire to drink, so stopped and had one.	Bored, frustrated, and worried.	'I've only got £25. So I can't do too much damage.'	I have borrowed money from flatmates or friends before.	'I can borrow money; and even if I only spent £25, I'd be strengthening a tendency to drink when feeling bad or bored.'	95
	Slightly elated from the alcohol, guilty.	'I can start afresh tomorrow.'	I have had this thought many times, and yet I found it extremely difficult to stop	'Past experience tells me that I'm unlikely to be able to "start afresh tomorrow". It isn't that	95

On one occasion recently, I went into a pub with the intention of drinking no more than two pints of beer. I drank four pints.	Bored, frustrated, and worried.	'I've got to drink more.'	On occasions, in the past, I have stopped drinking after a few pints.	...easy. First, the morning after, I'll feel terrible and want to blot that out. Second, I'll be reinforcing my tendency to drink.	90
	Slightly elated from the alcohol, guilty.	'Another few drinks won't do any harm'	On many, many occasions, in the past, 'another few drinks' has led to me losing control of my drinking and then getting angry with people.	Past experience suggests that I can stop drinking after two pints. I'll feel less guilt if I stop drinking now than if I carry on and no doubt behave badly.	95

drinking and stay stopped.

WORKSHEET 4B

IDENTIFYING AND CHALLENGING PERMISSIVE THOUGHTS ABOUT DRINKING

Trigger	Feelings and Sensations	Permissive Thoughts about Drinking	Evidence Not Supporting the Thought	Alternative Thought	Belief in Alternative Thought

					Rate how much you believe this thought to be true on a scale from 0 to 100.
				Note the alternative more helpful thought.	
			Use the eight questions on page 44 to challenge your thought.		
		What were you saying to yourself that made it easier to keep drinking? Highlight the key thought that makes you most likely to continue drinking.			
	What feelings and body sensations did you notice?				
When did it happen? Where were you? What were you doing? What were you thinking about?					

It is important to challenge your positive and permissive thoughts about drinking as often as you can. Make sure that you keep worksheets with you at all times. If you do drink in a manner that you consider unwise, record and challenge your thoughts as soon as possible after they've occurred. If you use these techniques on a regular basis you should find that as your belief in these positive and permissive thoughts decreases, your desire to drink in ways that aren't sensible will also decrease.

Don't be too harsh with yourself if you don't make progress as quickly as you'd like. Beware of expecting too much too soon. It takes time to create and believe in alternative thoughts about drinking, especially when you may be challenging a number of different thoughts at a time.

8

Dealing with Craving

Craving can be described as the desire to experience the effects brought on by drinking. It is almost inevitable that when you stop or reduce your drinking there will be times when you'll experience craving. Craving will reduce naturally if you don't satisfy it and, over time, you'll recognise that it is possible to manage it. Below are a list of typical things that might trigger craving.

Your Environment

Aspects of your environment, such as the time of day, day of the week, people you are with etc., can become associated with drinking so act as triggers.

Memories of the Drinking Life

Sometimes you may find yourself thinking of your drinking as a long-lost friend or partner and have thoughts such as 'A cold one really tasted good' or 'What's the point of going out in the evening without a drink?'

Negative Emotions

When you experience unpleasant thoughts or feelings, or when you're bored or stressed and finding it hard to find ways of enjoying yourself, you're more likely to experience craving.

Wanting to Enhance an already Positive Experience

Sometimes you may experience craving when you wish to make a positive experience even better. For example, you may have learned to associate drinking with socialising and think that drinking will make social interactions more 'enjoyable' and 'spontaneous'.

Techniques for Dealing with Craving

Coping Statements

When you feel strong cravings you may find it difficult to reason properly. Coming up with positive 'coping statements' can be useful to get you through a critical period. The following are examples of coping statements that can help reinforce your determination:

- 'I will put up a fight.'
- 'I'll feel healthy and not guilty in the morning.'
- 'Get the hell out of the situation now!'
- 'I can spend the money I will save on gigs, CDs, visits, or clothes.'
- 'I'll be taking responsibility for myself and my future.'

Try to think of examples of coping statements that might help you in critical situations and write them down.

Distraction

The key goal of this technique is to get you to shift the focus of your attention away from internal triggers (e.g. memories, moods, physical sensations and thoughts) and towards the external environment, so you're no longer thinking about your craving. Some techniques include:

- Describing your surroundings – Include anything that takes your fancy (e.g. a building, cars, shopfronts or people). Try to go into as much detail as possible.
- Talking – This may involve starting a conversation with a friend, a colleague or a family member.

- Trigger avoidance – Remove yourself from environments that trigger your craving (e.g. a pub, people drinking) by, for example, taking a brisk walk, visiting a friend or going for a drive.
- Household chores – Performing household chores will not only serve as distraction but will also help you boost your self-esteem because you've done something useful.
- Games – Playing games, such as board games, video games, cards or puzzles, can be quite challenging and will require concentration. In addition, you'll be able to play some of them by yourself so you won't be dependent on having other people around.

Review the Benefits of Sensible Drinking and the Costs of Unwise Drinking

Thinking about the benefits of sensible drinking and the costs of unwise drinking will weaken your craving. Look back at the worksheets you filled out in the last chapter and make your own personal list of both the benefits of sensible drinking and the costs of unwise drinking.

Decisional Delay

When you experience craving, try to put off the decision to drink for 20 minutes. Craving will usually be reduced substantially during these 20 minutes so you can remind yourself that it will not last forever.

Making a Flashcard

You can sum up all the information on how to manage your craving on a flashcard. Use your flashcard when you experience craving that you need to tackle quickly and effectively. An example of a completed flashcard is shown below:

Managing My Craving

Distraction (a) describe surroundings; (b) phone friend but don't talk about craving; (c) do chores; or (d) learn a poem or do a puzzle.

Coping statements 'Put up a fight'; 'I'll feel healthy and not guilty in the morning'; 'I'll avoid unwanted, dangerous, expensive behaviour'; 'I can spend the money I will save on gigs, CDs, visits, or clothes'; 'I'll not be creating financial, occupational, or emotional problems for myself'; 'I'll be breaking bad habits sooner rather than later, and be making life easier for myself'; and 'I'll be taking responsibility for myself and my future'.

Review the benefits of sensible drinking and the costs of unwise drinking: Benefits: feeling better; fewer money problems; better health and sleep: Costs: damages my health; costs me money; affects my job; it upsets my partner.

Identifying Apparently Irrelevant Decisions

During the course of a typical day you will make thousands of decisions. Some of the smaller and more ordinary ones may appear to have nothing to do with drinking. In reality these smaller and more ordinary decisions may lead you to drink in an unwise way. A useful exercise is to try to re-call these apparently irrelevant decisions. Think of a time, in the recent past, when you drank in an unwise way. Now, ask yourself the following questions:

1. 'What events and/or situation happened just before the drinking episode?'

2. 'Who was I with?'

3. 'Where was I and what time of the day and week was it?'

4. 'What decisions led to the drinking episode?'

5. 'What could I have done differently?'

6. 'What are the pros and cons of doing things differently?'

7. 'What will I do next time – what is the safe alternative?'

The following are examples of apparently irrelevant decisions that may lead to drinking too much:

*   Not making plans for the weekend.

*   Keeping too much alcohol at home.

*   Going to a party where people are drinking.

*   Going to the pub to see old drinking pals.

Use the worksheets on pages 70–75 to help you identify apparently irrelevant decisions that have led you to unwise drinking in the recent past. Worksheet 5A is an example of a completed exercise. Worksheet 5B is for you to fill out, identifying as many apparently irrelevant decisions as you can.

Once you've done this, repeat the exercise with any apparently irrelevant upcoming decision that you think may lead to drinking in the future, using Worksheet 6B again. An example of a completed exercise can be found on page 74 (Worksheet 6C). Remember that decisions may involve any aspect of your life, such as friends, recreational activities, family or work. In future, when faced with a high-risk option you should try to choose a safe alternative. If you need to enter a high-risk situation make sure you have a plan to protect yourself. For example, only go to a pub where you used to go to drink when you've rehearsed your drinking refusal skills.

WORKSHEET 5A
PAST APPARENTLY IRRELEVANT DECISIONS – JOHN'S STORY

Preceding Event/ Situation	Apparently Irrelevant Decision	What Could Have Been Done Differently?	Pros of Doing Things Differently	Cons of Doing Things Differently	Safe Alternative
Early evening. Working poorly. Felt low and frustrated. Recently found out ex-girlfriend has new boyfriend.	Aimlessly walking around central London, on my own.	I could have done some focused activity that would have given me pleasure (e.g. cinema, running).	Would have taken mind off work and girlfriend, and improved my mood.		Visit cinema or go running.
Morning. In bed. Felt low	Lay in bed for most of	I could have got up and	Would have halted the		Get up and go running.

and angry.	the day.	rot and lifted my mood.		Have plan for day that's manageable, not overwhelming, and includes activities to look forward to.
	immediately done something enjoyable and positive (e.g. running).			
	I could have had a manageable plan for the day that included things to look forward to.	Manageable plan would have increased likelihood of getting out of bed and made me feel better about the day, especially if plan included pleasurable activities.		

WORKSHEET 5B

PAST APPARENTLY IRRELEVANT DECISIONS

Preceding Event/ Situation	Apparently Irrelevant Decision	What Could Have Been Done Differently?	Pros of Doing Things Differently	Cons of Doing Things Differently	Safe Alternative

WORKSHEET 6C

UPCOMING APPARENTLY IRRELEVANT DECISIONS – JO'S STORY

Preceding Event/ Situation	Apparently Irrelevant Decision	What Could Have Been Done Differently?	Pros of Doing Things Differently	Cons of Doing Things Differently	Safe Alternative
Ross invited me to his wedding reception.	Accepted invitation.	Turn down invitation.	Avoid a risky situation.	It wouldn't be nice to miss his wedding reception.	Rehearse drinking refusal skills. Review motivation exercises. Leave early.
Parents have asked me to go on	(Option 1) Decline offer.	N/A	Avoid risky situation.	Greatly disappoint parents.	Discuss with Marcus. Accept, but,

holiday with them during winter break.	(Option 2) Accept offer.	N/A	Please parents and good for family.	Committed to risky situation without having thought things through.	prior to holiday, prepare myself (i.e. plan things to do on holiday, rehearse drinking refusal skills, and review my exercises).

10

Managing Setbacks

If you've managed to successfully work through this book you may be experiencing a growing sense of control over your drinking. This feeling will usually continue until you encounter a high-risk situation. Typical high-risk situations will include many of the triggers you may have identified previously (e.g. personal conflicts, feeling down, social pressure, time of the day, certain places, etc.). There are several things you can do to cope with these high-risk situations. These include: develop a personal summary of what you've learned from working through this book; keep clear in your mind why it is best to drink in a sensible way; work towards a balanced lifestyle; increase the number of enjoyable activities you take part in and learn to identify and cope with warning signals that precede high-risk situations.

Working Towards a Balanced Lifestyle

The degree of balance or imbalance in your daily life will have a big impact on your desire to drink.

The first thing to do is to ask yourself what areas of your life may need to be more balanced. These may include: work, exercise, your finances, relationships with friends, family and colleagues, nutrition and physical health. Think ahead over the next few months and list the challenges you may have to deal with in each of these areas. These could be related to starting a new job, moving house, sorting out your finances or the birth of a baby. Once you've done this write down ways in which these difficulties might be tackled. You may well need dedicated and specialist help to manage some of the difficulties you've identified.

Whatever you decide to do to make your life more balanced, remember to do it in a gradual way so as to avoid raising your expectations too much. As you begin to change your drinking habits you may well feel better and experience surges of energy. This may result in you taking on a variety of responsibilities in one go: getting a new job, moving into a new home, retraining, starting a big DIY project, cleaning out 20 years' worth of mess and so on. This enthusiasm can be a double-edged sword: it can be satisfying but also very tiring and unrewarding. At times, too much responsibility may end up leading you to question the value of drinking in a sensible way, so it is important to take on new responsibilities gradually.

Increasing Enjoyable Activities

If you don't have enjoyable 'normal' activities in your life negative emotions such as anxiety, low mood and worry will seem more obvious and important. This, in turn, will increase the chances of your wanting a drink. This is why it is crucial for you to engage regularly in pleasurable activities especially if you've made a commitment to drinking more sensibly, which will mean you'll not be relying so much on alcohol to try to improve your mood. Use the following steps to help boost the number of enjoyable activities you have in your life.

Step 1 Monitoring current enjoyable activities

The first step is to get accurate information on how much time you currently spend on enjoyable activities by monitoring them. You can do this quite easily by keeping a record of your activities during the week and rating how much pleasure you get from them. When completing your diary, make sure that you write down the activity you're engaged in and the levels of pleasure it gives you on a scale of 0 to 10 (where 0 is very little pleasure and 10 is a lot of pleasure). It is important you fill your diary in regularly so you can monitor the changes in pleasure you get from these activities during the course of a 4 to 6 week period.

Step 2 Developing a list of enjoyable activities

Once you've collected accurate information on what you're doing during the week, and what pleasure you get from your activities, you can begin listing enjoyable activities that you'd like to start or do more of. Try to aim for activities that are challenging (which may not feel so good at first) but become increasingly enjoyable and beneficial as time goes on. It is also helpful if these activities don't depend entirely on others, are non-competitive, have some personal value and can be improved with practice. Creative skills such as art, music and writing; physical pursuits such as cycling, jogging and swimming; hobbies, reading and relaxation are all good examples of the kind of activities that could be beneficial.

Step 3 Developing a schedule of enjoyable activities

Once you've a completed list of pleasurable activities you can start scheduling a small block of time each day (30–60 minutes) to devote to them. The goal is to *gradually* increase the activity levels and to maximise pleasure in the free time that you have available. You can begin this process by taking some time to sit quietly and review your list of pleasurable activities. You will probably not want to do the same thing every day. Schedule some time each day, but don't schedule the activity, so that what you do in your personal time doesn't feel like an obligation. When you feel that you've consistently managed to put aside the small block of time each day (30–60 minutes), you can gradually increase it to a more substantial block of time (60–120 minutes), if you have the free time available. Remember to keep your activities in manageable proportions.

Step 4 Comparing activity diaries

Once you've a completed list of pleasurable activities, and have scheduled and done them for a period of 4 to 6 weeks, return to your original diaries and compare them to your current diaries. Do you notice any differences? Scheduling pleasurable activities is one of the most powerful things you can do to improve your mood and at the same time reduce any unwise drinking.

High-Risk Situations: What to Do?

A useful technique to avoid returning to unwise

drinking habits is to know how to tackle high-risk situations. Ask yourself what high-risk situations might make you more likely to drink more and make a list of them. Once you've done this, write down what actions you would take to tackle them. An example of an action plan for tackling high-risk situations is shown below.

ACTION PLAN FOR HIGH-RISK SITUATIONS

Upcoming social event: 1. assess the risk ('Where?', 'When?', 'Who?'); 2. decide on whether to go; 3. rehearse my drinking refusal skills; and 4. maintain motivation by reviewing my blueprint for sensible drinking and continuing with enjoyable activities.

Old drinking pal: 1. avoid meeting where there's alcohol; and 2. only meet in a low-risk environment (e.g. coffee at lunchtime).

Bored with work: 1. remind myself that everyone gets bored with work sometimes; 2. do some more motivating work; and 3. schedule enjoyable activity (e.g. running or cinema).

Stressed with work: 1. remind myself that work is hard for everyone; 2. review opportunities for progression and support; and 3. schedule a pleasurable activity.

Craving: 1. use my craving flashcard; and 2. rehearse and practise strategies.

Coping with a Setback

If a setback occurs make sure you immediately put it in perspective:

It is not a disaster.

Rather, it is part of what you're trying to do: practise putting aside old drinking habits and replacing these with new and different habits. As with everything that needs practice it won't necessarily be easy, and there will be times when you'll have to pick yourself up and start all over again. What you'll probably find by persisting is that things get easier and that even if you do experience a setback a few times you won't think it is the end of the world and you'll get over it quickly. The following techniques for coping with setbacks may help:

- Stop what you're doing – If a setback occurs stop what you're doing and think about what is happening. The setback is almost certainly the consequence of not having properly acknowledged the high-risk situation.

- Don't panic – The instinctive reaction to a setback may be to blame yourself and feel extremely guilty about what's happened. This reaction is normal. Remember that all negative emotions eventually subside, including this one!

- Remember what you've achieved so far – Go back to your summary of the work you've done. Think back over the reasons that made you decide to change your drinking behaviour. Renew your commitment to change.

- Analyse the situation that brought about the setback – Rather than blaming yourself for the setback find out what happened. The setback was probably a one-off. Try to work out what led to the setback and what warning signals came before it.

- Kick-start the comeback – Review what you've accomplished and start again with the key techniques you know will work: remove yourself from high-risk situations and engage in pleasurable activities.

- Seek help – Ask friends, family or your partner to help you in any way they can. If you're alone seek help from professionals or self-help groups.

A Final Word of Encouragement

The strategies described in this book are intended to help you drink sensibly. On first impression they may appear straightforward and almost too simple. The reality is that using them successfully will take time and effort. In order to make the most of your efforts, as well as to keep track of progress, you should have easy access to all your diaries, worksheets and notes and take time to review them regularly.

You may be wondering whether it matters which of the techniques you start with. The techniques in this book follow a specific order and it is recommended that you stick to it. That said, the order is not fixed and you may find that starting with different techniques can also work for you. However, when you've decided which of the techniques to start with, make sure that you give it a fair go before you move on to a different one. It can be tempting to change a particular technique if it doesn't appear to be helpful at first. Stick with it until you feel sure you understand how it works. Try also to be realistic about the things you want to do. It is better to stick to small targets and be successful than to try to do everything in one go and feel you've failed. Don't forget that success breeds success, so it doesn't matter how small the success is that you start with. Make sure that when you've had one successful experience you don't leave things there, but try the same thing again. In this way you'll be able to build on your successes. Finally, it is best to start with smaller tasks and to tackle harder ones once you've built your confidence and know more how the techniques work for you. I hope you've found this book helpful and wish you the very best of luck in achieving your goal of sensible drinking.

Other Things that Might Help

This book has provided you with an introduction to sensible drinking. Some people will find that reading this book is all they need to do in order to see a big improvement, whilst others may feel that they need a bit more information and help, and in this case there are some longer and more detailed self-help books and programmes around. Ask your GP if there's a 'Books on Prescription' scheme running in your area – if there is not I'd recommend you read:

Overcoming Alcohol Misuse by Marcantonio Spada

Overcoming Stress by Lee Brosan and Gillian Todd

Overcoming Worry by Kevin Meares and Mark Freeston

Overcoming Depression by Paul Gilbert

Sometimes the self-help approach works better if you have someone supporting you. Ask your GP if there is anyone in the surgery who would be able to work through your self-help book with you. For some people a self-help approach may not be enough. If this is the case for you then there are other kinds of help available.

Talk to your GP – make an appointment to go through the available different treatment options. Your GP can refer you to an NHS Cognitive Behavioural Therapy practitioner. Don't be put off if you've not found working through this book right for you – talking to a Cognitive Behavioural Therapy practitioner can make a big difference. If an NHS Cognitive Behavioural Therapy practitioner is not available in your area or you would prefer not to wait to see one, ask your GP to recommend a private one.

Although Cognitive Behavioural Therapy is widely recommended for problems to do with alcohol use there are other kinds of therapy available which you could also discuss with your GP.

Medication may also be helpful for some people and sometimes a combination of medication and therapy can work well. However, you need to discuss this form of treatment and any possible side effects with your GP to work out whether it is right for you.

The following organisations can offer help and advice on alcohol use and misuse and you may find them a useful source of information:

Alcohol Concern

Tel: 020 7566 9800; email: contact@alcohol concern.org.uk

Al-Anon Information Centre

Tel: 0800 9177 650; email: help@alcoholics-anonymous.org.uk

British Association for Behavioural and Cognitive Psychotherapies (BABCP)

Tel: 0161 705 4304; email: babcp@babcp.org.uk